A MORE VALUED
SUCCESS

A MORE VALUED SUCCESS

Paul S. Spitale

iUniverse, Inc.
New York Lincoln Shanghai

A MORE VALUED SUCCESS

iUniverse books may be ordered through booksellers or by contacting:

iUniverse
2021 Pine Lake Road, Suite 100
Lincoln, NE 68512
www.iuniverse.com
1-800-Authors (1-800-288-4677)

Because of the dynamic nature of the Internet, any Web addresses or links contained in this book may have changed since publication and may no longer be valid.

The views expressed in this work are solely those of the author and do not necessarily reflect the views of the publisher, and the publisher hereby disclaims any responsibility for them.

ISBN: 978-0-595-47863-7 (pbk)
ISBN: 978-0-595-71389-9 (cloth)

Printed in the United States of America

The author will honor some special people in his life by donating 20% of all profits to the following noble causes:

- *Juvenile Diabetes Research Foundation*
- *National Association for Autism Research*
- *The Rodman Ride for Kids*
- *Dana-Farber Cancer Institute*

Contents

Highlights from Valued Success ...

- If we're not making choices and decisions based on who we are or what we'd like to be, what are we basing our decisions upon?

- We are truly satisfied when we are value driven, not task driven.

- Our values are the cornerstone and the roadmap of our lives.

- Worry debilitates us while working within our values liberates us.

- We are responsible for acting within the framework of our values.

- All the talk, all the statements, all the writing, and all the roadmaps are meaningless if you take the wrong turns.

- Remember, winning at all costs is not truly winning at all. It's both the winning and how you play the game that ultimately leads to your fulfillment.

- The values that we hold are infinitely more important than winning.

- You must believe in your self-worth—you are valuable, and there is no more important principle of life than the values you hold true.

- Companies must strive for a healthy diversity, using individual team members with various skills and talents working in the same framework of values.

- All companies move in varied directions. Successful companies move in step with their values.

- Live your values.

Introduction

Years ago, as an executive focused on improving both my career and family life, I became obsessed with books, CDs, and videos, hoping to learn as much as I could about developing a successful career and a fulfilling family life. I found that the most common self-help materials fall into one of three categories: sales axioms, motivational materials, and educational materials. Although each can be effective, they are limited because they do not consider the reader's *values*. All people are different, driven to make decisions by their own experiences and upbringing. The beauty of my program, Valued Success, is that while it fills a void in the self-help market, it also works in harmony with other self-help materials. Because of my knowledge of the market and competitive materials, combined with my professional experience and education, I feel uniquely qualified to write this book.

Over the last twenty-five years, I've built many highly successful teams. Currently, I'm a senior vice president for Sony Electronics. I've been with Sony for more than two decades. I've written this book for many reasons, but after working successfully in the highly competitive field of consumer electronics, I wanted to share some of my most personal insights on business today. While working at Sony I went on to complete my masters in business administration, then went on to Columbia University, where I graduated from their 2004 Columbia Senior Executive Program.

My approach is simple and incorporates the most frequently used corporate strategies to reach objectives. Traditional strategic planning follows five steps: (1) mission, (2) corporate objectives, (3) strategy, (4) implementation, and (5) review. I've added a very important element to the five key areas of the traditional strategic planning model taught at MBA programs all over the country: And that element is values, *Valued Success* planning follows the following five steps:

1. Values and Mission Statement

2. Identifying Core Objectives

3. Valued Strategic Solutions

4. Valued Action

5. Success Analysis

With the added element of *values*, we are able to customize this program to suit our personal objectives and life's ambitions. I will briefly explain each of the five areas in this introduction, explaining them in detail in later chapters.

Step one, the creation of the Values and Mission Statements, which is pivotal and is probably the most difficult and time consuming to complete. This process challenges us to look inward at what we truly value, not only understanding those values intuitively but articulating them. Once you have done this, you are on your way. You will write what is valuable to you in the context of the five following areas: your home, your close friends, your spiritual relationships, your work, and finally a fifth category, which I call "physical." Physical could be made up of special activities, hobbies, and other things outside the workplace and home that you participate in.

By asking ourselves key questions (detailed later in chapter 1) as they relate to these five key areas, we can identify the things that make us tick and answer the question, "*What is really important to us?*" It's a tough question but one that can be answered. The process of developing a Values Statement can take a few months or up to one year. This statement will become the roadmap for our life's decisions.

After we have completed the Values Statement, we will turn our attention to *purpose*. What is the main purpose for the organization, its *mission?* This is the key question we need to answer when creating a Mission Statement. This statement may be about winning or adding shareholder value or developing a method of serving customers, but most importantly, it will need to be clear and concise. I suggest only one or two sentences, which will ensure a clear message that will be easily communicated throughout a firm or family. Mission or Purpose Statements are high-level looks into a company's "future state" or the reason for the firm's existence. After creating both a Values Statement and a Mission Statement, you are ready to start creating Core Objectives.

Core Objectives are the areas in our lives that need our *valued attention*. These are not areas that we cannot possibly influence but rather those where we can improve or enhance ourselves. Another important part about Core Objectives is getting down to the *root cause*. For example, an unloved child can develop many problems symptomatic of a greater core problem, but until that child deals with that core issue (the inability to feel loved) and actually *is* loved, the child will likely have many other problems. The child could become a truancy problem in school, become drug or alcohol dependent, or develop an angry personality. All these things may be symptoms of that root cause, the feeling of neglect and of being unloved.

The next step is to examine Valued Strategic Solutions. At this stage, we will look to people with similar problems and, most importantly, people whom we value and admire. These individuals can be our parents, relatives, friends, business colleagues, or other individuals we value. We will look to them for advice, developing our own solutions and integrating brainstorming ideas around what we truly value. Then we're going to look at techniques for channeling our ideas into one Valued Strategic Solution to attack one specific Core Objective. The plan of attack should be simple. If there are too many steps, the road to completion will become a blur. The more unclear the strategic plan, the less chance we have for a successful outcome. In my approach to creating strategic solutions, I don't recommend any more than five steps. And obviously, the strategy itself, as well as the actions in the strategy, must be based on our values.

Let's review the first three steps of the Valued Success program. We begin with creating Values and Mission Statements that we believe in. We move on to developing Core Objectives, areas in our lives that need our valued attention and that we can influence. Then we develop a Valued Strategic Solution to remedy one area, by developing a strategy based on our values.

The fourth step, taking Valued Actions, is probably the easiest, once we've established what we want to accomplish and how. At this point, we must proceed with caution. This is where the potential for disaster can arise and people fall into the "win at all costs" trap. Most people who win in that manner do it at the expense of their values.

The final step, Success Analysis, asks two basic questions. First, in terms of results, did we get what we needed? Second, did we act within our values? Remember that winning at all costs is not winning at all; it's both the winning and how we play the game that ultimately leads to total fulfillment. In fact, *the values we hold dear are infinitely more important than winning.* This statement represents the essence of the Valued Success program.

I'll write later about my father, but let me now describe him briefly. My father is someone who I would describe as a grounded person and full of value. He has chosen to lead a very principled life. He's not the wealthiest man in the world, although he has a fair amount of wealth and has always been a good provider. As a merchant for over thirty-five years, he's not a man of fame or extreme power—in fact, if you measured his life in business against those of the industry giants, he's probably had a more quiet existence—but what my father has, no one can ever take away from him: he has lived his life by the principles he holds important. My father places high value in his family, hard work, and honesty. My father also has the highest level of affection for his wife and his children. Nothing can ever take that away from him. He is truly a Valued Success and works at it every day.

Throughout our lives, we've all known people who just seemed a little bit happier, a little more grounded, and we ask ourselves, "How can I be more like this person? Why can't I be happier?" Most often, this happens for one of two reasons: either the values most important to us are not at the forefront of our consciousness or we are simply not acting upon the values we know to be true and right. There are literally millions of people in psychotherapy each year—some very successful, wealthy, and famous—who veered away from what they truly valued to acquire wealth, fame, or power, things they *thought* they valued! Money is not the enemy, nor is fame or power. The enemy, these feelings of not being as satisfied as we could be, starts to surface any time we stray from our personal roadmap, our values.

If we are not making choices and decisions based on who we are or what we'd like to be, what are we making decisions upon? This program gives you the tools to help put perspective and direction into your life. It is your turn to read the material, get an understanding of the process, and work through each step carefully. This is an easy process, but you will need to give yourself time to reflect on your life. Also, the steps will keep you focused so that each one is manageable.

Valued Success is not a quick-fix program. It is designed to put our values at the center of all our actions. Once completed, it produces an all-encompassing life change. This book doesn't promote empty promises or lucrative real estate deals to make us richer than we imagined, but I promise that when we honestly assess what our principles are—and do the necessary work to start acting on those principles—we will find our lives to be more meaningful. We will start to feel more important, because the things we say and do will represent who we are. People will notice and react positively, because we will have become one of those people we used to admire from a distance—a person who takes actions based on his or her true values.

Although the Valued Success program is designed for individuals, it is also possible to share these principles with our friends, companies, and families. By making our Values Statement visible, displaying it in high-traffic areas (in our homes for example), we provide a constant reminder of what we believe in. In our own home, my wife and I have a framed print on our wall that lists our Family's Statement of Value. When we have problems or things to work out as a family, we refer to that list and develop our strategy, because through that list we can develop a more Valued Success.

I would bet that if you asked a sampling of middle management employees at most *Fortune* 500 companies two simple questions, they wouldn't know the answers: (1) what is your company's Mission Statement? And (2) what are your company's objectives? The result of not knowing these things are discord, companies heading in one direction and uninformed employees heading in all different directions, insubordination, frustration, unhealthy diversity, and lack of competitive advantage. Ideally, all companies would share their values and principles in a way that gave all employees a clear sense of the company's mission and objectives.

I wrote this book for many reasons. First, I wanted some way to show my family, in a very meaningful way, how much I value the work that I've put so much time into. Second, I wanted a way to share with other people and organizations the feeling of contentment and absolute fulfillment that occurs when we work, live, and act according to the principles we believe in. Finally, after all the time and energy I spent studying self-help materials, I uncovered things that fell beyond my understanding. Some authors, despite their brilliance, were either too driven by sales axioms or too caught up in academic language that the average person would not understand or find useful. The Valued Success program can reach everyone, is simple to understand, and is founded in the values that you define as important. If you follow it step by step, it will make your life a true Valued Success.

1

Values and Mission Statement

The Values Statement is the most important part of the Valued Success program. Although it's a five-step program, the first step allows you to clearly identify and look at your life in a new way. We're going to go through some exercises to give you some ways to organize your life so you can decide what is truly important, what things you truly value, and what you ultimately stand for. Then you'll make those values a part of your daily actions and decision-making.

Today, business and family leaders lack values from which to lead. Decisions based on crisis and emotion seems to be the order of the day. Many families are being torn apart because there is no leadership, direction, or values in the family unit. Our corporations are being politicized in such a way that no one individual knows which direction take or which team to be on, because there is no sense of mission, purpose, or corporate value. Individually, our lives are so caught up in emotion and crisis that we lack a clear understanding of who we are and what we believe in, which is much more important than all the outside influences we have to deal with. Therefore, step number one (creating a Values Statement) is finding out what we truly think is important. Give yourself ample time to cultivate a personal Values Statement that accurately reflects your true core values. You or your company may need up to six months, or even as much as one year, to create a Values Statement.

When creating your Values Statement, think of how a contractor builds a home. If he rushes his material purchases, he is likely to forget some key items. If he rushes the home plans, he might miss reviewing special features that the buyer wants or needs. If he rushes his subcontractors, their workmanship may suffer from inconsistencies and low quality. The result is that the home is built with the wrong materials, the buyer does not get his preferred features, and the work is of poor quality. If the contractor had put the time and effort into building this home, the product would have been dramatically different.

Likewise, please don't rush the process of creating a Values Statement. You'll find that by doing the first step thoroughly, that you will be set up to get more fulfillment from your personal and corporate undertakings.

The first step (creating a Values Statement) is to break your life into five key parts:

1. **Home**—"a dwelling place together with the family or social units that occupies it; household … a valued place regarded as a refuge or place of origin."[1]

2. **Friend**—"a person whom one knows, likes and trusts … one who supports, sympathizes with or patronizes a group, cause or movement."[2]

3. **Spiritual**—a person's faith, belief in an afterlife, or a belief in a higher power.

4. **Work**—"the means by which one earns one's livelihood; a trade, craft, business or profession."[3]

5. **Physical**—any special activities, hobbies, sports, reading, or any other forms of enjoyment outside the daily grind of work.

Ask yourself the following questions with regard to each of the five areas previously listed:

1. What do I believe in?

---

1. American Heritage Dictionary (Boston, Massachusetts: Houghton Mifflin Company, 1985).
2. Ibid.
3. Ibid.

2. What do I think is important and why?

3. Who or what do I love and why?

4. What values have I learned through my experiences?

5. What values do I aspire to have?

You will find that by asking these questions, you will begin to build a framework of your own personal values. These specific questions will enable you to pinpoint the most important values in your life. It's important to remember that you must answer these questions with complete honesty and openness. By answering openly and honestly, you will develop an insight into your own personal core values.

Sample of a completed exercise, taken from the author's Values Statement planning

1. What do I believe in?

- at home: honesty with all family members, kindness, forgiveness

- with friends: give unconditionally with friends, be a supportive friend

- at work: hard work can overcome a lot, be persistent, a team player not an island

- spiritually: prayer can reduce my life's stresses

- in a physical context: the body should rest only when tired

2. What do I think is important and why?

- at home: family activities, a family that stays and plays together loves one another

- with friends: effort, I will never lose a friend for lack of effort

- at work: timeliness, you can't count on an untimely employee and I want my fellow workers to count on me

- spiritually: commitment to prayer, it makes my days more meaningful and satisfying

- in a physical context: commitment, to enjoy or get any benefit from hockey you must put the time in

3. Who or what do I love and why?

- at home: my wife, she is the most loving person I've ever known, she always brings a smile to my face, she's the light in my life

- with friends: forgiveness, if I make a mistake I hope my friends can forgive me as I would forgive them

- at work: I love making other people's workload lighter

- spiritually: my parents, who gave me strong values from which to live

- in a physical context: my father, who at age 70, is a living example of the axiom "an active life is a happy life"

4. What values have I learned through my experiences?

- at home: never stop loving my family

- with friends: good friends are hard to find and easy to lose, never lose a good friend

- at work: never judge a book by its cover; always take a second look

- spiritually: with prayer comes confidence

- in a physical context: the more I exercise the better I feel, the better I feel the more I exercise

5. What values do I aspire to have?

- at home: to be happy, upbeat, and understanding 99.9% of the time

- with friends: always be first to forgive

- at work: always ready to help any other co-worker—"I'll make time"

- spiritually: make decisions with God in mind

- in a physical context: never give less than 100%

By answering specific questions in these five areas of our lives, you will begin to develop your roadmap. You will start to formulate a structure of who and what you truly value, and more importantly, why. This process is a soul-searching exercise. There will be no easy answers—you may have a long or short Values Statement. I suggest a short Values Statement consisting of eight to ten bullet-point items. The reason is, if you have a four-page text (accurate as it may be), you might find it difficult to use in your daily life, where you must sometimes make decisions in matter of moments.

For example, if you are on the phone with a client or talking to a child, you may find it hard to come up with a quick, accurate response concerning the issue at hand when you must refer to a four-page statement of values.

I spent four years volunteering at an orphanage in Southern New Hampshire as a Big Sibling. One of the directors of the facility, David Applegate, struck me with his ability to counsel the children. My little brother and many of the other kids feel that over the last four years, Dave has been there. He has been the most responsive and the most timely, while providing the best and most straightforward answers of all the counselors. He always has the kid's best interest at heart, and the feeling is mutual among all the staff at the children's home.

One day I asked Dave, "How do you stay focused on the children?" As I sat in his office, I noticed a picture. The picture was of his family. Dave told me, in a very private moment, that his family was very close and that all the good in his life came from the devoted love of his mother and father. He has a portrait of his family on his credenza, and he uses that picture much in the same way you will use your Values Statement. Use your Values Statement as a visual reminder of what is important, what you value, and how you can impart those values onto your daily situations.

One summer day, two years ago, Dave was approached by two young girls at the orphanage about going to the movies. Dave asked who was driving. The girls replied, "A friend from Manchester, NH." He informed the youths that they could only go with a Big Sibling or staff member. The two girls didn't understand why he was being "so unfair." He told them that his actions were in their best interest. He reminded them of a teenager who had gone missing in Manchester, NH, on a similar trip to the mall. Despite their disappointment, the children knew Dave's commitment to his values, and they knew that his decision was based in those values.

Dave won't allow himself to be swayed because of a child's priorities. He needs to do what is best for the children, and he knows and trusts the values set forth by his parents. The portrait in his office means more than the paper it is printed on. That portrait stands for the values he believes in. As a result, he has become a value-centered individual whom I would consider a *valued success*.

As you can see, a Values Statement is a very powerful tool. Much as Dave's picture represents his parents and his values, a Values Statement helps you stay focused on what you deem important.

The qualities of an effective Values Statement of value are as follows:

a. It must accurately express the persons or company's true values.

It would not make much sense to cultivate a Values Statement that incorporates someone else's true values. It must come from within your family or organization.

b. It must be written and it should be reviewed frequently.

If you write it down and it collects dust on a shelf, it serves no purpose. Your Values Statement must be like Dave's picture—a daily reminder, reviewed often as part of your decision-making process.

c. It must be visible and accessible in your surroundings.

If you are a telemarketer, put it near your phone at work. In your home, keep your Values Statement in a high-traffic area for all the family to see. Some ideas for displaying a Family Values

Statement: on the refrigerator, next to a bedroom mirror or wherever the family gets a chance to get together and focus on what is important. This Values Statement will help guide the members of the family to start making decisions based on their own values.

d. It must be reassessed and reviewed every two years.

You want to make sure that the information is still accurate, and you will always want to look for ways to make improvements in your life. You will find that your values are timeless and will not change from year to year. However, a change in core values may follow a seminal event, such as a debate with a close relative, a separation or new relationship, a job promotion or termination, the birth of a baby, or the loss of a loved one. However, I think you will usually find that your values are timeless. If you find your values changing 180 degrees over short periods, you may want to re-examine whether those are truly core values. Rather, was your value based on emotional or political content? It's important to realize that these things we hold most important are the cornerstones of our actions in the Valued Success program.

I have a very close friend named Jim Mastromatteo. He has always been the type of person who was very focused and driven towards his personal goals. He has always known what he wanted to do in life, and made valued choices as a young man to insure his life's work would be aligned with his values. We've been friends for over thirty years and I've always felt that Jim had a sense of purpose, a value from which he made his decisions. Jim, even in high school, had a strong sense of helping others. He had a way of always extending himself to help or befriend others. In high school he told me that he wanted to be a physician, when very few of our friends knew exactly what they wanted for a career. In this regard, Jim was extremely focused.

Sure enough, after we finished undergraduate schooling, Jim was accepted into medical school and has since gone on to become a successful Radiologist. He is committed through his values and core principle of dedicating his life to helping people. This commitment carries over into all facets of his life in how he helps his family, brothers and sisters, and his patients. He is a star in my life and a living example of what Valued Success can be. Jim is a person whose core value of helping people is at the forefront of his actions. That is what Valued Success is all about.

Because the Values Statement will become the cornerstone of your actions, take plenty of time to write its contents. We need to use the Values Statement as a roadmap and as a reference tool. How many times have we driven into an unfamiliar city or town not knowing which road to take? Often we need to refer to a map or ask a local resident for directions. How can we go through life without our own customized roadmap? How are we expected to make life's tough choices without the ability to access our personal core values roadmap? That is the purpose of a Values Statement. It gives us a way to tackle difficult situations in our lives, and as mentioned earlier, it's not uncommon to take up to six months or longer to formulate a Values Statement.

I'd like to share a story about a value-oriented person, Abraham Lincoln. He lived a life of Valued Success. He is a shining example that the values that you hold, if you make them a part of your actions, will mark you as a person with integrity, honesty, and more importantly, a person driven from true purpose. I would like to review some of the content of two value-driven speeches Lincoln gave. The first was given to his attorney general on April 4, 1864, when Lincoln said, "I am naturally anti-slavery. If slavery is not wrong, nothing is wrong. I cannot remember when I did not so think and feel."[4] Lincoln's statement reflects his awareness of his internal core values. He had always felt that slavery was wrong and was faced with making a decision based on that value.

---

4.   Gorton Carruth and Eugene Ehrlich, *American Quotations* (New York and Avenel, New Jersey: Wings Books, 1988), 515.

In another speech Lincoln delivered on July 10, 1858, Lincoln said, "I leave you, hoping that the lamp of liberty will burn in your bosoms, until there shall no longer be doubt that all men are created free and equal."[5] Lincoln is saying that his belief in human liberty was at the cornerstone of his actions. This shows his commitment to living his sense of value.

We need to look to our close relatives whose opinions we most value. For me it is my parents; for you it may be an aunt, uncle, cousin, or grandparent. My father, more than anyone else, is the impetus for my putting this book together. He is not a man who tells people what he believes; he shows them.

My father has a complete and undying belief in hard work. While growing up, he engaged our entire family not just with his words but with his actions. If you or someone you know works in the retail industry, you understand that long hours are part of the game. My father retired as a successful merchant after more than forty years. One of the reasons for his great success was his work ethic. He worked long, tireless hours and weekends, continuing to push the idea that hard work is at the core of what he believes. I have seen that through his work, many positive outcomes have occurred. He has been able to sustain a family of four children and a wife, enjoy his grandchil-

---

5.   Ibid., 515.

dren, and take part in his children's accomplishments and disappointments. I've never known my father to do anything in a lazy or apathetic manner, whether it's mowing the lawn, working on a strategic plan for his business, practicing tennis, or just preparing a family dinner. He is a living example to me of what hard work can do. I asked him once, "Dad why do you have such a strong belief in hard work?" My father answered by pointing to a photograph of my grandfather, Carl Spitale. With this action, he was showing me that his values came directly from his father.

Together with my wife, we have taught our children that when they take on projects or get involved in something, they shouldn't be afraid to work hard. There is satisfaction that comes from working as hard as we possibly can, if we believe in what we are doing. This belief in hard work was passed down from my grandfather to my father and from my father to me. It's commendable that my Dad has strong personal values and core principles, but it is more important for him to see his children become successful and productive adults. One of the reasons that our family is a success is that my father was so committed to his personal values.

Another person I counseled with and interviewed when developing my own Values Statement was my younger brother Mark. Mark is one of the most optimistic people I've ever met. The reason for his optimism is that Mark was diagnosed at age three with juvenile diabetes and has had to cope with an unpleasant medical history all his life. He depends on two injections of insulin daily and has to watch his diet and health carefully. He received laser treatments on his eyes to correct his eyesight problems, which have come as a result of his diabetes. For most, a medical condition like this would interfere with maintaining a positive outlook on life. But aside from these challenges, my brother looks at life the way a painter looks at a sunset. Some look at a sunset and say, "that's the end of another day," but my brother savors the beauty in the colors of the sunset. He always sees the best in the people, places, and the challenges placed before him.

The reason for his optimism is sometimes unclear to me. Although I'm not as optimistic as Mark, I do believe in and admire his proactive approach to life. Nothing brings me greater joy than seeing Mark challenge a problem or take on a project, because he has the spirit and undying commitment to achieving a positive outcome. He also lives a life filled with Valued Success. He has never let his physical problems hinder his life in any way. Mark is active in many sports, has a great career as a sales professional, and has a full social calendar and good friends. He is married and has a family with whom he can share his optimistic outlook.

Although we cannot always live exactly according to our values, your Values Statement should represent both who you are and who you aspire to be. What do we value? By doing the exercises and interviewing close friends and relatives, you will begin to see a development of your own special core values.

Early in my career, I worked with a department manager at the Dayton Hudson Department Stores, which later became Marshall Field's Department Stores. He was labeled a jack-of-all-trades and master of none. This was true, but what he lacked was not creativity but rather a belief in the value of hard work. He was a great idea person, but had lacked follow through and dedication to stay with a project to completion. I asked him one day, "Why don't you enjoy the projects that you work on? Why, when they become difficult or take a little extra effort to finish, do you lose interest and walk away?" He said, "I don't know. I just get to a point where there's no enjoyment, no interest." I started to think, that's a truly reactive way to deal with life's problems. I told him that when he feels like quitting, he needs to refocus and look at what hard work has done for others in the organization. I also told him there were many "hard workers" in the company that were not nearly as talented as he was. After talking and getting to know him, he admitted an empty feeling when leaving a project and said if he could finish a project successfully, he might feel more accomplished.

Later on, I learned that he had stepped up to the challenge and put his career on track. In two years, he became one of the most valued executives in that store. The reason was simple: once he determined that there was a premium placed on working hard, all of his decision-making changed.

To change behaviors we must change the value we place on a segment of our lives. Without that, our lives will become an emotional roller coaster, because there will be no value or importance placed on you. When you really think about it, what are values? They are a reflection of who you are and of what you would like to become. If you're not making choices and decisions based on who you are or what you'd like to be, what are you making decisions upon? You can't live according to how others would like you to act. Going through life with somebody else's ideals is not part of any Valued Success. The key to success is to find something you like to do, sell yourself to it and work hard. Gary Player said, "The harder you work, the luckier you get."[6] Do you know why? He valued practice and hard work and as he was working, he felt good about acting in his value. Luck had very little to do with Gary Player's success.

Now that we've created a strong set of values, it's time to create a Mission Statement. This statement should keep us focused and pushing towards our preferred future. As a rule, the statement should be only one or two sentences.

---

6.   H. Jackson Brown, Jr., *A Father's Book of Wisdom* (Nashville, Tennessee: Rutledge Hill Press, 1988), 10.

Make it clear and concise so it can be communicated throughout the organization. If you are a member of the New York Yankees, your mission is clear and concise each year: "to win the World Championship." As the most successful professional franchise in sports, their leaders have done a wonderful job of articulating their organizational purpose. You don't need to like the Yankees to respect the clarity with which they state their corporate mission. Any company that has a strong set of values from which to operate and a clear and concise mission has a good chance of being a Valued Success.

Let us review ...

- First, segment your life into five areas and then ask the five key questions.

- Second, talk to close friends and relatives whose opinions you value and admire.

- Third, look internally and reflect upon what you think is important, as well as who you are.

- Fourth, write eight to ten bullets reflecting your values, which will serve as your Values Statement.

- Fifth, create a clear and concise Mission Statement, which will define the purpose for your organization.

Give some thought to this analogy. If your best friend were to say a few words on your behalf, what would he or she say? What do you think would surprise you? On the other hand, do you think you know yourself completely? When we set up a Values Statement, we must have a true and accurate understanding of who we are. If we have values based in negative principles or ideals, we need to weed those out and replace them with new, positive ideals. By doing this and following the steps of the program, you will simplify your life. The hardest part of each day is making decisions; after all, how can we choose between right and wrong if we haven't researched ourselves? Once you take the time to write down a Values Statement and a Mission Statement, your decision-making process will become much simpler. You will have a clear roadmap and an accurate reflection of your core values.

I'll leave you with a thought. When taking the first step in the five-step Valued Success program, you need to remind yourself of this statement:

We are truly satisfied when we are value driven, not task driven.

STORY OF PURPOSE—PAT RILEY

Professional basketball head coach and winner of five world championships

Riley writes in his book, *The Winner Within*, about covenants: "an agreement that binds people together. Sometimes it is written out in great detail. Sometimes it is unspoken, completely expressed through action or trust."[7] When Pat talks about covenants, you could substitute our Values Statement. He goes on further to define a constructive covenant as one that,

- binds people together

- creates an equal footing

- helps people shoulder their own responsibilities

- prescribes terms for the help and support of others

- creates a foundation for teamwork[8]

Riley is aware that no Valued Success can come to anyone unless the entire person, team, family, or corporation is committed to working with a sense of purpose. Without values, we, like many teams the Lakers played

---

7.   Pat Riley, *The Winner Within* (New York: G.P. Putnam's Sons, 1993), 57.
8.   Ibid.

in the 1980s, become sailing ships without the benefit of a rudder. Without your seamanship, your ship is being steered by the wind and the currents.

There are many very talented teams in the National Basketball Association that are perennial losers. Why? I suggest it has less to do with their playing talents and more to do with not having a statement of purpose. Coach Riley's ability to get his personnel committed to an ideal would make him a successful leader in any area of endeavor. He is truly a Valued Success.

2

Creating Core Objectives

Creating Core Objectives is to define the issues in our lives needing valued attention. When we think of objectives, things that we strive for, goals that we may have set, an objective is a very specific area of our life and needs intense effort to reach a particular outcome. And thus, turn into what I have defined as a Valued Success, once the objective is achieved. I've chosen the word core as it defines being at the center or root of the objective. Anytime we are faced with a problem in our lives, we often just scratch the surface, because we are so caught up in an emotional process. As a result, we end up just fixing the symptoms of a deeper core problem.

Let me give you an example. I once had a school classmate who was a peculiar youngster. He didn't seem to enjoy school, although at times he showed brilliances. He seemed to be easygoing, but somehow he always caused a ruckus. He always caused problems while going to school, drawing attention to himself. I always felt that there was something behind his unusual behavior. As I talked to him during our school days, I realized that he had a poor self-image and that this manifested itself in his behavior at school. He was always causing problems when there was nothing going on. He really became a problem. I asked him one day, "What is troubling you?" I asked him knowing that most people can't see and don't realize the causes of their actions. But as we talked further, he expressed some resentment towards his parents, who had just recently divorced. He resented the whole process; felt abandoned and unloved, and feared that he was less important to one or the other parent. His problems weren't in the classroom but rather within himself as a result of his situation. He was unable to cope with his feelings of loss and abandonment over the divorce.

In this case, if his teacher merely treated the symptom (acting up in class), by using corporal punishment or sending him to detention, a place where he would get even less attention and feel more abandoned, what would be the result? I think the results would be quite the same, if not worse: his attention-getting activities would become even more pronounced. I suggest that unless one dealt with the root cause, his feeling of being unloved, there would be no change in his outward behavior.

The above is an example of how we should define a root cause. This is to make certain that you're dealing with an issue that will bring a dramatic valued change. Don't get caught up in changing circumstantial and secondary problems. Fix the root causes, your Core Objectives. Don't just put down a laundry list of hit-or-miss objectives. Try not to make the mistake of listing thirty specific goals that you would like to accomplish in the next four months. Nobody can give focused attention to thirty different items in a three- or four-month period. Spend more time and write out a shorter, more focused list that you can put all your valued effort into.

There are two important elements of any objective. The first is an *internal element,* one that should always be based on your values. Chapter 1 discusses developing a Values Statement, by detailing the things in our lives that are important to us. It is important that we understand our objectives, and our Core Objectives must fit with who we are as a person. For example, if one of your objectives is to become a physical therapist, but you place no value in the medical profession of helping people with physical problems, you will likely have trouble attaining that objective, since your value system does not support it. Our values are the cornerstone and roadmap of our lives, as stated in chapter 1. If our objectives are not completely in alignment with the things that we value, we won't find any satisfaction in achieving these objectives. Show me a person who has gained great wealth by cheating or lessening their values, and I'll show you a person who takes very little comfort in his fortunes.

The second, *external element* relates to the results that we desire. The internal element deals more with our values, how we feel about a particular objective and whether it fits in with our values. However, the external element deals with the results we wish to attain. You cannot have an internal element without an external, but as I will suggest throughout this project, the internal element is the most important. If you acquire something by means not in keeping with your values, the result will be feelings of emptiness; the character of the person who achieved that particular empty victory will begin to break down. Remember: the internal and external elements go hand in hand. The internal elements of either an objective or a strategy are always far more important than the external results we wish to achieve.

Let's discuss some of the key elements that make up a strong Core Objective. I am a firm believer that a strong Core Objective must be written. People who have clear, written goals and objectives find reaching those objectives a much easier task than those who have not written them down at all.

As I was watching the Masters Tournament a few weeks ago, I noted how much information a PGA professional has to process before he swings a golf club. The process is similar to writing your Core Objectives. The golf professional wants to know the exact yardage, even pacing it off if he has to. He also gets input from a caddie, finding out the exact pin placement on the green, slope of the green, cut of the grass on the green, and wind conditions. He then funnels all this information and visualizes the particular shot he would like to make. As if he were writing down an objective, he writes down in his mind the result he wants to obtain and then reinforces it, taking a practice swing while always remembering the objective. As he hits the ball, there's a rush of enthusiasm. Where would that professional golfer be without knowing the yardage or visualizing the target, without judging the wind or practicing a swing, without the advice of a caddie or competent golf professional? How would he strike that ball and hit the shots that most of us dream of? There is no way, and there is no luck involved—everything he does, in terms of practice, preparation, studying, and visualizing and writing it down, is similar to what we'll do in setting Core Objectives.

The exercise of writing down our objectives makes it clearer and lets us visualize the potential outcomes. It's an automatic process—as you write it down, your mind will already be thinking about strategies to obtain it. Likewise, when a golfer picks up a blade of grass and throws it in the air; he's anticipating the shot and thinking about how he can deliver the desired result.

So, the first step is to write it down. Secondly, it's important that we make the objective as clear and concise as possible—no more than one sentence. I had a good friend in graduate school who had a list of thirty goals that he wanted to achieve by age forty. I had a hard time providing any constructive criticism, except to say that his reasoning and approach were thoughtful. Then I thought, with so much information to look at, it would be very difficult to focus on what was important. I contend that if you have two, three, or four paragraphs detailing one objective, you are likely dealing with a symptomatic problem (remember the example of the misbehaving classmate) as opposed to a Core Objective.

My advice on setting Core Objectives is not to work on more than four objectives at any one time. This will keep your efforts more directed and more consistent with your values. As I mentioned earlier, if you had thirty or forty goals to work on in your job, could you really stay focused throughout the day? Could you realistically spend your time thinking creatively and working out particular valued strategies and approaches to fix seven, eight, twenty, or twenty-five goals in your life? It's important, at any one time in your life, to stay focused on working with only one to four goals, or Core Objectives. Once an objective is achieved, you may add another Core Objective to your list.

Let's review some of the main points regarding Core Objectives. We talked earlier about Core Objectives and the fact that they are issues in our lives that need valued attention. If these were issues that didn't need our valued attention, things beyond our control, worrying about them or fixating on them wouldn't be productive. An objective keeps us driven and focused on what *is* important to us. Why should we worry about things in our lives that don't need our valued attention? Does worry solve anything? Does worry bring comfort? All the worrying in the world just hurts and infects our chances of reaching a higher level of performance. I suggest that often worry debilitates us, while working within our values liberates us.

Remember to make your Core Objectives very specific, keeping them to no more than one sentence. We also discussed the reasons for choosing the word "core," meaning the root cause, so not dealing with secondary, symptomatic problems. We discussed not setting hit-or-miss objectives and working on no more than four at any one time. I believe once you write a Core Objective, you should work within your own values as diligently and as hard as you can to attain it. Until you do, it should continue to be part of what you aspire achieve. I don't believe there's any value in a person saying at the end of a year, "Well, I achieved twelve of fifteen objectives this year—it was a good year." I don't think the number dictates whether someone has a good or bad year. If seven or eight of the twelve objectives didn't even fit within your values and the other six you didn't work in your values to attain, I'd say it was a real poor year. However, if you choose four

Core Objectives and worked diligently within your values to attain them, you would find fulfillment, a Valued Success you would really be proud of.

Also remember that there are *internal* and *external* *elements* when setting Core Objectives. The external elements are the results you desire, while the internal element relates to how the Core Objective fits into your values (outlined in your Values Statement).

If you do a good job setting Core Objectives, you will find that you can become the architect of your own life. Just by writing down what you wish to achieve, your strategy will begin to emerge. Just as a golfer walks up to the ball on the fairway and visualizes the opportunities, you will become liberated and feel the comfort of purpose and direction once you write down your Core Objectives.

STORY OF PURPOSE—ARNOLD JACOB AUERBACH

Led the Boston Celtics to sixteen world championships since 1950

Arnold Jacob Auerbach, better known as "Red Auerbach," took over as coach of the Boston Celtics in 1950 and went to 39-30 in his first year on the job. They also made the playoffs the next five years.[9] Red's objective since arriving in Boston in 1950 was to play hard every night and, ultimately, to win world championships. No one other than Auerbach could have dreamed the success of the next ten seasons, as the Celtics went on to win nine of ten world championships.[10] Even though the team from 1950 to 1955 did not win a world championship, they played hard, in accordance with the values Auerbach instilled, known as "Celtics' pride."

In 1956, the objective was the same, but one important element was added—Bill Russell, the greatest winner in professional sports history. Remembering from this chapter, there is both an internal element tied directly to our individual, team, or group's values and an external component tied to the results we desire. For Red and Bill

---

9.   Dan Shaugnessy, *Evergreen: The Boston Celtics* (New York: St. Martin's Press, 1990), 7.

10.   Ibid., 8.

Russell, the objective was clear—to win every time the Celtics took the floor and ultimately win championships. When the history of basketball is finally written, I'm sure there will be plenty to say about Red Auerbach's Valued Success as a professional coach, general manager, and person.

3

Creating Valued Strategic Solutions

To start the process of creating a Valued Strategic Solution, you must first look to the advisors in your life. Seek out individuals who have dealt with similar Core Objectives and have a similar value structure to your own. By consulting with these individuals, you will begin to see the wisdom of their experiences. From this, you will begin to develop ideas and strategies for achieving Valued Success and more successful outcomes.

When seeking your valued advisor (a colleague, friend, family member, etc.), be certain that it is someone in whom you trust and who shares your values. Perhaps you admire the way they go about solving problems or reaching personal objectives. Once you have learned about their strategy and the way they have attacked a similar objective to your own, all you need to do is model their behavior. Envision yourself creating a strategy based on the success of their valued experiences.

The second thing that you can do is to draw on your own experiences. Reflect on how you can design and implement a Valued Strategic Solution to the day-to-day problems you face; these solutions will be created out of your own experiences and values.

Next, assemble a group of individuals to work on the solution. Group members can be family, friends, members of a study group, or business associates—anyone who has experiences to share. Use these people to brainstorm ideas and solutions to the problems you are facing. Some people find it hard to brainstorm. Generally, brainstorming should be a free flow of ideas to reach a particular objective. Let the ideas flow freely without discrimination or judgment, at first. It's best to gather lots of information from which to work, so you can later apply the best strategies when creating your own personal Valued Strategic Solution. By allowing a free flow of ideas, you will get more creative input from the group members. If the group starts discriminating or favoring one idea vs. another, the brainstorming session will probably be less creative, less original, and ultimately less successful—which will diminish the quality of the input you are looking for.

Rules for brainstorming

1. Keep the group size between three and eight people.

2. Present a theme or objective.

3. Put one person in charge of recording all ideas.

4. Discourage any judgments among group members; there will be no right or wrong answers, good or bad ideas; all ideas will be welcomed graciously.

5. Place a time limit on the session; five to ten minutes seems to work best.

The next step in creating a Valued Strategic Solution is processing the data from the previous steps. The goal is to narrow down all the information to one solution that best fits your Core Objective and is in alignment with your Values Statement.

Recap to creating a valued strategic solution:

1. Consult with valued advisors, people with commonly shared values and objectives.

2. Reflect deeply on your internal values and experiences to begin developing internal strategies.

3. Use brainstorming techniques to gather other possible Valued Solutions.

4. Filter through the previous three steps and implement the Valued Strategic Solution that best accomplishes your Core Objective and aligns with your Values Statement.

The key to a Valued Strategic Solution is that the actions and the strategy must be based in your values. As an example, the NCAA has very strict recruiting and specific regulations around collegiate athletes and scholarships. Just imagine a college basketball team whose coach had set a standard of excellence through the values of hard work and fair play. The team excelled and was invited to the NCAA tournament and went to the Final Four. The team was sky high, firing on all cylinders; they won the semi-final game and went into the finals, ultimately clinching the national championship. It was a dream come true for both the athletes and the coach—the pinnacle of success in collegiate athletics; and then what? It was revealed through one of your alumni associations that two of the key players had been getting paid as if they were professional athletes. So the coach won the game, but you didn't uphold the NCAA standards set forth by the university. More importantly, this team lost sight of its Values Statement, set forth by that team for the year.

You wanted to be a successful team, have a winning season, and ultimately play for a national championship and win, but only through the values of hard play while keeping with the principles and regulations of the NCAA. As a coach of that team, that national championship trophy would become nothing more than a symbol of an empty win. Although you won a trophy and the game, you did it through a means that was not in keeping with the team's values. This is the key to a Valued Strategic Solution. The strategy that you set forth must be in keeping with the values you hold.

I also believe that the strategy should be written out and have a finite term. Our strategies must have a beginning and a completion time. The completion time is important because it allows us to re-evaluate. I suggest that no strategy is clear-cut. Most good strategies evolve as our experiences become more sharpened and our values become deeper and more convincing. Time limits help us make those changes and re-evaluate the objectives we are trying to accomplish.

Many people have strategies that don't need to be written. And there are many successful people who have lived, worked, and acted according to their values but never used a written Values Statement or strategy. But most of us cannot do this. I suggest that by using a written strategy, you improve your chances for success. As an example, if you are trying to make Grandma Spitale's world-famous spaghetti sauce, your chances for success are much greater if you use the written ingredients and cooking instructions (strategies) she wrote down and passed on to the family years ago. Numerous studies have shown that people are ultimately more successful if they have a clear mission and written objectives. Without a written objective and strategy, individuals find themselves sailing in an ocean without the benefit of a rudder, just flailing around without any direction or purpose.

This leads to another important point. The solution itself should not have too many parts. My golden rule is no more than five parts. The more complex you make your plan; the more difficult it will be to accomplish your goals or any Valued Successes.

Imagine a person who likes the game of golf taking a lesson. Now, when she goes out to play, instead of thinking about one particular objective she would like to accomplish on the course, and maybe one or two simple strategies to effect a change, she thinks about fifteen to twenties strategies around the golf swing. What happens? She has no concept of what a golf swing is; instead of simplifying the strategy, she has made the process more difficult and complex, and ultimately she turns away from the game. So, lest you become like the golfer with too many axioms or the business person with too many objectives, remember to keep it simple—no more than five parts in any winning Valued Strategic Solution.

The actions in your strategy must be value based (remember the NCAA coaching example). Also, the strategy itself must be value based. For instance, if you're about to begin a project that's going to involve long hours (upwards of eighty per week) of intense labor, and you've developed a strategy that says, "I think I can get this project done in six weeks," let me just say this: if you're not someone with a strong work ethic and include hard work as a core value, your strategy is going to be in direct discord with the actions needed to accomplish the goal. Be honest with yourself. If you are not prepared and don't place any value in working those kinds of hours, you can assume that your strategy will fail and the results will be less than successful.

Make sure your strategy is realistic. This doesn't mean that it needs to be easy, but you do need to have the tools and resources to accomplish the Core Objective. It makes no sense to state an objective that you are either ill prepared to complete or incapable of completing. Do not end up relying on someone else's efforts to complete the job. Make sure that your objective and strategy puts you in sole ownership of its accomplishment. If you try to put forth an objective that relies on a team of individuals and the team doesn't have the same Core Objective, your strategy is not realistic. You can't determine the outcome based on the team's talents, because they won't be as committed to the outcome as you are. So make sure your strategy is realistic and that you have all the proper resources to meet the Core Objective.

For example, if someone said that he wanted to become a medical doctor within two years but only had a high school diploma, would it be realistic to think he could achieve this goal? No, because the time needed is much greater than two years. For someone to become a medical doctor, he or she must successfully complete four years of undergraduate school, four additional years of medical school, and one or two more years of an internship program. In total, it is a ten-year process to become a medical doctor. A person with this strategy is not basing it upon the schooling or the steps needed to accomplish the objective, the results once again would be less than successful. To set up a strategy around being a doctor in two years with those circumstances is not possible. This strategy is not based in any sense of realism.

Another key element of a strategy is an unrelenting commitment to a positive outcome. We define a positive outcome as a successful outcome based in our values. I will talk further in chapter four about having what I call a positive self-dialog. When attacking any Core Objective, you must commit to making the outcome as close to your values as possible, meeting your Core Objectives exactly as you have written them down. If you have an unrelenting and unwavering commitment to your values and to your strategy, your chances for success will escalate.

Let's do a quick review on creating a Valued Strategic Solution. To start the process we need to look at three basic areas. We need to consult valued advisors and model their behavior. We need to do an internal reflection based on our own personal experiences and values. Then, if we have access to a group, it may be helpful to create a brainstorming exercise. Finally, we need to take all three areas of input and reduce the data collected from the proceeding steps and create one list. Choose one strategy that will best attack your Core Objectives while keeping in alignment with your values.

Key points to remember in creating valued strategic solutions:

1. The actions in our strategy must be based in our values. (Remember the example of the collegiate basketball team and how their success was shown to be lacking true value.)

2. The solution must be time-based and written down.

3. Our strategic solution can't have too many parts, no more than five. The more complex we make it, the more difficult to execute.

4. Not only our actions but also our strategy must be based in our values. (Remember the example

of the person who was not committed to hard work but developed a strategy based on working eighty hours a week to accomplish a goal.)

5. The strategy must be realistic and supported by the proper resources to accomplish the Core Objective.

6. Finally, you must have an unrelenting and unwavering commitment to positives outcomes.

By using these approaches, you will find yourself creating better Valued Strategic Solutions to life's opportunities.

STORY OF PURPOSE—WINSTON CHURCHILL

England's most famous political and military leader

Winston Churchill had a firm belief in freedom and self-governance. He was filled with a personal conviction for human freedom and the value of free human expression. He had the challenge of trying to save the entire free world, taking on Hitler's war machine in the European theater. He turned his appeal to the English people, the United States, and President Roosevelt. When saying, "Put your confidence in us, give us your faith and your blessing and under providence, all will be well, we shall not fail or falter, we shall not weaken or tire, neither the sudden shock of battle nor the long drawn trials of vigilance and insertion will wear us down. Give us the tools and we will finish the job!"[11] Churchill's objective was simple: to fight back the threat of Nazi Germany and keep whole England and its free ideals.

With his values clearly in place and a Core Objective of keeping England whole, he was now ready to map out a Valued Strategic Solution. To that end, he decided to meet with President Roosevelt in the North Atlantic sea. During the meetings, Churchill, surrounded by hun-

---

11. Winston Churchill, *Churchill in His Own Voice*, Caedmon Audio, CPN 2018, audiotape one, side B.

dreds of British and American troops and with President Roosevelt at his side, said, "When I looked upon that densely packed congregation of fighting men of the same language, of the same faith, of the same fundamental laws, of the same ideals and now to a large extent the same interests, and certainly in different degrees facing the same dangers—it swept across me that here was the only hope but also the sure hope of saving the world."[12]

One thing is clear: without the alliance between Britain and the United States, "standing shoulder to shoulder with President Roosevelt" as Churchill put it, the war and the world would look very different than it does today. Churchill's Valued Strategic Solution included an important alliance with the United States, a country he felt valued freedom similarly. Churchill was a man of true purpose and a Valued Success as a leader.

---

12. Ibid.

4

Taking Valued Actions

Before looking at the fourth step in the process of creating Valued Success, let us do a quick review of how far we've come. We started our journey with the building blocks, a roadmap, where we would lay out all the groundwork, that being the creation of our Values Statement. From there, we studied and defined the issues in our lives that needed our valued attention, which led to creating Core Objectives. From our Core Objectives we turned to creating Valued Strategic Solutions to meet these objectives. Now, we have done all the necessary preparation to complete the fourth step, taking Valued Actions.

As I reflect on the subject of taking Valued Actions, my brother Tom comes to mind. Tom is an independent, value-driven individual. He has always seemed to act with a sense of principle. My brother loathes people who say one thing and do another. For him, there is no other way than to act with a sense of personal honor and integrity.

After graduating from the University of Wisconsin, he worked for a large bank in the Minneapolis area. Although he excelled there, I felt it would only be a matter of time before he set out to become self-employed. Sure enough, within two years, he entered into a partnership with a friend who shared similar values to his own. Together, they currently own a small moving company. Until my brother could fully express his values in his actions—his work—his career (no matter how successful) would be misaligned. The only way for him to feel he was a Valued Success was to work in a structure with the same values and core principles that he had. I believe only then could he or anyone else find true comfort in an organizational setting. I would also suggest that Tom's life is not much different from all of our lives, in that we are most content working within the framework of our values. His spirit, which seemed always to refuse any compromise to his values, is one that shines to me as an example of personal honor and integrity.

The moment you take Valued Actions is when your plan either succeeds or falls apart. Even the best plans, if not acted upon in accordance with the values that we hold to, will fail. You must ensure that all your actions align with your Personal Values Statement (or that all your corporate actions align with your Corporate Statement of Values).

How many companies have we seen that value frugality and expense management? How many companies send the message that expense reductions are essential if they are to stay in business? However, if you were to audit the middle, upper, senior executive branches of their company, often you would find extravagant expense budgets, flying privileges (sometimes on private planes), and other questionable expenditures. A company that values expense management but spends excessively is an example of a company misaligned with its corporate values and objectives.

When a company's (or individual's) actions do not align with its values, the results are always lacking in value and purpose. Somehow, the company has gotten lost between the creation of its Corporate Statement of Value and the actions the firm is executing. These employees decided that their actions would not be in keeping with the principles the company holds near and dear, those special values that represent what the company is (or would like to become). The Corporate Values Statement is merely a piece of paper, if the employees fail to act with the essence of its stated value.

Let me give you another sample situation. For the longest time I used to ask my grandfather why he smoked. He couldn't give me an answer; he had smoked for such a long time that his habit was more of an unconscious addiction than a conscious choice. In his later years, he became ill and was told by a physician that if he valued his family and his life, it was time to change this behavior. He would need to quit smoking cigarettes. Now I know after smoking for nearly fifty years, it must have been one of the hardest things he ever had to do. Nothing else could have gotten him to change this behavior. When the doctor put his condition in the context of family—which my grandfather loved, honored, and respected—he was forced to ask himself every time he opened up a cigarette box and every time he lit a match if he was acting in defiance of his values. There is no stronger motivator than the values we hold. I am happy to report that my grandfather, at the time, quit smoking.

Whether you're planning for a corporation, family, or individual, step four in the process of creating Valued Successes is the easiest, because there's not nearly as much thought involved with taking Valued Actions. This step can also be the most challenging, because it calls our personal convictions to the forefront. We can no longer hide behind excuses, temperament changes, outside influences, or the manic episodes within our family. Now we are challenged to act in accordance with the framework of our values.

At the end of this chapter, you will read another story of purpose. The story is about Nixon's presidential administration, which was brought down politically in the mid-1970s. The most telling thing about this event in history is that it illustrates the responsibility of each member in a team, family, or corporation to act within a sense of value. The actions taken at the Watergate Hotel were certainly not representative of the values or purpose to uphold the public good. The administrators, assistants, cabinet members, and operatives that were involved in this covert activity, and the subsequent cover-up, played a role in something valueless. It can be said that Mr. Nixon bore the brunt of the scandal, as did his close cabinet members, who served actual jail terms. It is important to realize that it's not enough simply to set policy or create solutions that fit in with our values. It's not just enough to attack and to put out objectives that we think can be reached through our values. Only through Valued Actions can we say that our ideas and solutions have truly worked.

The most important steps in taking Valued Actions:

1. All your actions, corporate or individual, must be tied directly to and be in conjunction with your Personal or Corporate Statement of Values.

2. You need to create a positive self-dialog—you must become like any high-performing athlete and not be surprised by your success but rather become experts in expecting success and successful outcomes.

Many psychologists talk about scripting—the dialog that plays out in our minds, sometimes positive, sometimes negative. It's important that we focus in on having positive self-dialogs, especially when attacking the Core Objectives in our lives, the issues that need our valued attention. If our esteem is lacking or if our purpose is less than valued, we will start to have a negative dialog, with thoughts of "I don't think I can do that" or "Are you sure you want to try that?" Have you ever seen the end result with someone who has a negative self-dialog? We must push these negative thoughts aside and concentrate deeply on creating a positive self-dialog. Envision a positive outcome, every time.

I was watching a golf tournament this summer and was amazed at the concentration shown by Tiger Woods. Tiger is on pace to catch Jack Nicklaus for the most major victories in professional golf, which today sits at eighteen. When you see this young man block out all outside factors—the money, the crowd, the wind, the pressure—and simply step up to the shot and wins the tournament, you can't help but be amazed at that level of focus. What's true for great athletes like Tiger Woods or Michael Jordan is also true for business executives. They must block out the noise and focus on their Mission and Core Values and then take Valued Actions. Seeing the target (which is aligned with our values), taking Valued Actions, having a positive thought process, and creating a positive self-dialog to reach that feeling of elation when a Valued Success is achieved are all parts of the process. Complete success, fulfillment and gratification that fills Tiger Woods when that ball goes into the hole and he wins the tournament —could only be equaled by the picture of success that Tiger Woods paints within his own mind.

We may not win a golf tournament for hundreds of thousands of dollars, but in our own way we can expect success the same way Tiger expects those pitch shots to go in. When world-class runners break speed records, you can bet that their world-record pace was just a product of Valued Actions and a dream they envisioned using positive self-dialog. They see it, they visualize it, and they envision themselves running as fast as they possibly can. With that, they break records, set new marks in creative advancement, and ultimately set a standard of excellence for others to strive for. Taking Valued Actions can be easy, but like everything else in life, it becomes easier the more often we act according to our values. When my grandfather quit smoking, I'm sure the first day, first week, first time out for dinner when he couldn't have a cigarette, it was a habit he missed greatly. The decision not to smoke became easier over time, as his confidence grew, and knowing he made the right decision helped him act according to his values. He probably thought to himself, "I must continue to uphold my health and support my family." All the talk, all the statements, all the writing, and all the roadmaps are meaningless if you take the wrong turns. It would be as if you were building a home and the first thing you did was took a house plan (call this a Values Statement), then went and bought all the materials, using only materials that fit in with your architect's plans (call this your Core Objectives), then met with the contractor and went over the plans (Valued Strategic Solutions) to get the house built, and finally when it came time to build, hired an incompetent labor force. A labor force that was inexperienced, incapable, and uncommitted to carrying out the architect's plan. What would such a home look like? Conversely, what would be the result if you hired competent, highly effective, and positive individuals using the same materials and the same plan to build the home? As you make the effort to act in your values, you will find that it's easier and more gratifying. If you elect not to act according to your values, you will find just the opposite. You will most likely experience a lack of fulfillment and continual frustration. In the case of corporations, failing to act on corporate values will likely result in a political, mistrusting corporate culture faced with financial hardships. In the case of families, you will face uncertainty, separation, and dysfunctionality. Why? Because the individual or team lacked the ability and sense of responsibility to act within the values that they set out to uphold, and the outcome was less than optimal.

I would also suggest that these values exist whether you write them down or not. The reason for getting them down on paper is to help individuals and corporations more readily access them.

The most important message in this book is this: we are called to live our values. That really is the sum of the Valued Success process, and it is what this book teaches us to do. The central theme of Valued Success is to put your values first, at the forefront of your actions and strategies. Live your values.

STORY OF PURPOSE—RICHARD MILHOUS NIXON

Thirty-seventh President of the United States, born 1913; president from 1969 to 1974

Sometimes a story can show the proper method by illustrating and showing mistakes of the past. In the Watergate scandal, we saw an administration widely held to be the best foreign policy makers of this century brought down politically. It would be hard to blame one person or group for the cover-up at the Watergate Hotel. In his own words, detailed in Nixon's book, *In the Arena*, he writes of the scandal. "As I wrote my memoirs, I was able to look back at Watergate and separate myth from fact. At the core of the scandal was the fact that individuals associated with my re-election campaign were caught breaking into and installing telephone wiretaps at the headquarters of the Democratic National Committee in the Watergate Hotel. After their arrest, others in my campaign and in my administration attempted to cover-up this connection in order to minimize the political damage. I failed to take matters firmly into my own hands and discover the facts and to fire any and all people involved or implicated in the break in."[13]

---

13. Richard Nixon, *In the Arena* (New York: Simon and Schuster, 1990), 33.

It is clear that at some point, the Nixon administration took on a win-at-all-costs mindset. After reading this chapter, you can see that even if the press and Mr. Nixon's political adversaries had not brought the matter of Watergate to the American public, the actions taken by the administration were at best valueless. Even if these actions had not been revealed, their results, good or bad, would still be unsuccessful and lacking in value.

5

The Success Analysis

At this point, we can reflect upon the four previous steps in the Valued Success process: (1) Values Statement, what we value or aspire to be, (2) Creating Core Objectives, issues in our lives that need valued attention, (3) Valued Strategic Solutions, game plans created in accordance with our values, and (4) taking Valued Actions, acting within our values roadmap. That brings us to the point where we can begin the review process. The most important part of this step is creating an accurate measure of what we needed to accomplish, one that will help us determine our successes and what a Valued Success is. In simple terms, we will evaluate our success on the two below listed measures:

1. **External Element: Did we get what we needed in terms of results?**

2. **Internal Element: Did we act according to our values to achieve the desired results?**

These questions can be used to measure any corporate, family, or individual success. For example, Wal-Mart's goal was to become America's largest retailer. They attained this, and they were able to do it while maintaining their corporate value, running through all levels of the organization, of making their customer number one. They created a corporate culture to give the customer what they want. I think it's easy to say that they did just that. Their associates have acted according to the values set out by the company and Sam Walton. Therefore, Wal-Mart could be considered a Valued Success, as well as a very successful organization.

I would like to discuss a very special person in my life, my mother. My mother is a person with a deep commitment to helping people and has devoted her life to medicine by working as a registered nurse. And like my friend Jimmy (Dr. James Mastromatteo, discussed earlier), my mother has always felt a personal obligation to work in a career that helped people who were sick and aided people who were hurting. My mother set goals in life that were in keeping with her personal values—raising a family and helping the sick, both of which fall into accordance with her values. Her career choices as well as her ability to love unconditionally and to help whenever needed all make her a Valued Success as a person. These qualities are all in perfect alignment with her personal values.

Not everyone wins national basketball championships or has the opportunity to run a multibillion dollar corporation like Wal-Mart, but everyone has the duty and responsibility of looking at themselves, their work groups, and their corporations and finding out what they truly value. Following this self-realization, one should go out and put into practice what he or she believes to be truly important.

Another person who has touched my life greatly is Sue, my sister, who, like my mother, also had a vision of helping others. She went to school to become an educator and is now employed at a private facility that handles children who are wards of the state and have come from broken homes or have no families to speak of. These semi-private facilities are the only home some of these children have ever had. Prior to this job, I saw my sister work painstakingly for over two years at an orphanage, helping children from age four through eighteen. Just watching my sister, I could see that her work was more than just a job. This job allowed her to live and express her personal value of helping others. This position empowered her to work diligently every day at something she believed in.

A few years back, she reached a turning point and made a tough decision. Although it was emotionally gratifying to work at the orphanage caring for these parentless children, she decided to take a job in retail. She could make more money as a very bright, hardworking, young professional. She could create a promising future in the business world if she wanted it, and she felt it was time take her life in a new direction. After only ten months in retail, while learning and becoming a well-respected executive, she decided it was most important to incorporate her values into her work. Her work in retail did not fulfill her values toward human kindness, educating, and giving of herself to others who needed her love and attention. Despite more lucrative opportunities in retail, she resigned and went to work for a facility that handled abused children. This new position has been great for her and she has worked her way up to regional director, a highly regarded position. She is very happy doing this work, and no amount of money, no amount of fame, could take away her success and personal contentment. She is able to give her heart to those children, and that's all that matters.

Both my mother and sister feel fulfilled, because they are acting according to their values and succeeding in helping others and making a difference in people's lives. Nothing can match the feeling of elation my sister feels when one of her children at the facility does well in school. There is no match for the gratification my mother gets when a patient leaves her office feeling better than when he or she came in. I bet that feeling of joy and excitement is similar for anyone else who has envisioned a success and worked hard to accomplish a goal.

Not all Valued Successes have to be grand events, like making a perfect shot in golf or winning world championships in basketball, but even simple feelings of accomplishment can be considered the most valuable successes.

Remember, winning at all costs is not truly winning at all. It's both winning and how you play the game that will ultimately lead to your total fulfillment. In fact, the values you hold are infinitely more important than winning. If you're not making choices and decisions based on who you are or what you'd like to be, what are you making decisions upon?

Let me close with a story of value about Wal-Mart Stores and Sam Walton.

STORY OF PURPOSE—SAM WALTON

Founder of Wal-Mart Stores, Bentonville, Arkansas; born 1918, died 1992

Samuel Moore Walton is one of the most successful retail merchants of all time. He was able to mobilize an entire company around one driving theme: "The customer is number one."[14] To Sam, and the workers in the Wal-Mart family, this was not just a hollow gesture but rather a central Statement of Values that ran throughout the organization. The interesting thing about Wal-Mart's success story is that in every area of the company—from store administration, warehousing and logistics, to computers/MIS, and purchasing—Wal-Mart employees are working to make their customers number one. "A question asked by Sam at many Wal-Mart store and corporate gatherings was, 'Who's number one?' And the response from the entire group was always an enthusiastic, 'The customer!'"[15]

Here's what some other industry leaders had to say about Sam's Valued Success:

Harry Cunningham, founder of K-Mart Stores
"Sam's establishment of the Walton culture throughout the company was the key to the whole thing. It's just

---

14. Sam Walton and John Huey, *Made in America* (New York: Doubleday, 1992), 157.
15. Ibid., 157.

incomparable. He is the greatest businessman of this century."[16]

Roberto C. Goizueta, former chairman and CEO of Coca Cola Company
"Sam Walton understands better than anyone else that no business can exist without customers. He lives by his credo, which is to make the customer the centerpiece of all his efforts. And in the process of serving Wal-Mart's Customers to perfection, he also serves Wal-Mart's Associates, its share owners, its communities, and the rest of its stakeholders in an extraordinary fashion—almost without parallel in American business."[17]

The reason I bring this story to your attention is that, in the simplest terms, by sticking to his vision of giving customers what they want, Sam's company became the biggest and most successful retailer in the United States.

After reading this story, let me ask you two important questions. Did Wal-Mart and Sam reach and exceed their business objective? Yes. Did Sam and the employees in the Wal-Mart family achieve their objectives through its value of making the customer number one? Yes again. Is Wal-Mart a Valued Success? Yes.

---

16. Ibid., 156.
17. Ibid., 173.

6

The Power of a Positive Mental Attitude

In our power to think positively comes the resource to unleash our own personal potential. Visualizing a positive outcome is tremendously liberating as we break through the negatives in our minds and create a positive value driven outcome. Anthony Robbins, a world class motivator says, "if we form a representation that things will work, than we create the internal resources we need to produce the stat that will support us in producing positive results."[18] As humans, we are given the mind power to choose one or another approach in all areas and situations in our lives. No person, no condition, no climate can make you or anyone else have a bad day. You have the power to choose your response to any situation. How many individuals do you know that let all sorts of outside influences infect their outlooks—bad weather, car trouble, children, and relationship problems, to name a

---

18. Anthony Robbins, *Unlimited Power* (New York: Ballantine Books, 1986), 44.

few? If someone adopts a poor or negative outlook, he or she is bound to have a very long, unpleasant day. In the Valued Success program, there is no room for doubt or worry. We must change any negative internal dialog with an internal, positive, purposeful, value-driven response.

We've all seen winners and we're sometimes tempted to say, "Boy, are they full of themselves." The irony is, they probably are, because they probably learned early in life that the only way to accomplish any task is to first believe in and envision one's own success. This ultimately leads to more positive self-dialog and highly successful outcomes. Having a positive mental attitude and developing better self-dialog is tremendously empowering, but it is not the key to success. By using the Valued Success approach, in concert with a strong and positive mental outlook, your chances for success are terrific.

Someone, whom I've learned a great deal from, through his books and recordings, is Zig Ziglar. He details in his book *How to Be a Winner* that "he frequently encounters people who are enormously confused about the subject of positive thinking. They often think we positive thinkers believe with positive thinking we can do anything. That's ridiculous. Positive thinking won't let you do anything, but it will help you do everything better than negative thinking will."[19]

---

19. Zig Ziglar, *How to Be a Winner*, Simon and Schuster Audio, 52063-6, audiotape one, side A.

In taking on any objective, if we remember to act according to our values and implement positive visualization toward reaching our goal, even when our results don't meet our high expectations, we'll likely be in a better position to succeed—with an even stronger valued strategy due to this first attempt. Denis Waitley, a nationally acclaimed author and expert in the field of human psychology, says, "Failure is the fertilizer of success."[20]

This reminds me of a story from last summer. I was playing golf in a heated family title match. The entire day I had set forth an objective for myself—to carefully read each putt and visualize each putt going in the hole, and to block out all negative images before actually striking the ball. On the seventeenth hole, I had a one-stroke lead and a ten-foot downhill putt to increase my lead to two strokes with one hole to play. This putt was the entire match. As I approached the putt, I was going through my pre-shot routine, and then it hit me, "Boy this is a tricky downhill putt; if I miss it; I could three-putt from only ten feet." Talk about a negative self-dialog. Before I started that putt, I should have handed my brother the family title. Well, you guessed it. I three-putted and the match was all even heading into the final hole. We both reached the par four in two shots and my ball landed about twelve feet away from the hole, and once again it was above the

---

20. Denis Waitley, *Being the Best*, Nightingale-Conant Audio, 712CT, audiotape, side A.

hole. My brother was approximately twenty-five feet and lagged his first putt to less than one foot and tapped it for a routine par. The match turned to me; now my mental approach was critical. As I approached these downhill's putt and going through the very same pre-shot routine, then in came a negative visualization. I thought, "If you miss this putt, you could three-putt again and this time lose the match." With this thought clearly in my mind, I decided to back away. I closed my eyes and redirected my thoughts to a new visualization—of a beautiful rolling putt down into the hole for the family title. As I opened my eyes, I felt as if I had made the putt and won the family title. Then I actually stroked the ball in. The feeling of success was overwhelming. I remember that match to this day, because for me it's an example of how positive self-dialog can make any outcome a bit better. That day it was the difference between winning and losing.

Thomas Edison once said, "I am not discouraged because every wrong attempt discarded is another step forward."[21] This book is all about moving forward with a sense of value and a positive outlook.

Ken Blanchard, world-famous co-author of the bestselling book *The One Minute Manager*, explained in a new effort entitled *Everyone's a Coach* (co-written with Miami Dolphins ex-head coach Don Shula), "World class ath-

---

21. Anthony Robbins, *Awaken the Giant Within* (New York: Simon and Schuster, 1991), 42.

letes often visualize themselves breaking a world record, making a perfect game, or a 99 yard punt return for a touchdown. They know their power comes from having a clear mental picture of their best performance potential. People are more likely to follow something they can clearly see."[22] This visualization is important to any positive self-dialog, and no person or condition can distort a perfect visualization unless you allow negative thinking to corrupt your outlook. You must believe in your own self worth. You are valuable. There are no more important principles of life than the values you hold true. Take a bad situation and create opportunities to learn; take a good situation and create even higher expectations of success.

Another key to a positive mental attitude is to surround yourself with positive and enthusiastic people. I'm learning a lot as a father with three young children. One thing I've learned is that when children play together in playgroups, if one child has a cold it's not too long before the entire playgroup has a sore throat and a cough. This cold is like people with negative attitudes. The more you hang around them, the more they seem to affect your outlook. My father-in-law had a saying: "Show me your friends and I'll show you who you are." In his mind, there was no value in establishing relationships with people who wouldn't enhance your own positive perspective. Looking

22. Ken Blanchard and Don Shula, *Everyone's a Coach*, Harper Audio, CPN 2342, audiotape one, side A.

back on my life, I can honestly say there is a lot of truth in his words.

Denis Waitley also said in his book *Being the Best*, "We can't let others set the standards for our successes or failures,"[23] and "If it is to be, it's up to me."[24] Our goal in living the Valued Success program is to enhance the value of our lives. If we rebound from adversity with confidence, based in our values and a positive mental approach, we will start turning losses into valued wins. We must continue to push our values forward and focus on taking up Valued Actions, not time.

---

23. Waitley, *Being*, side A.
24. Waitley, *Being*, side B.

7

Other Areas of Value

The Family Structure

Our families, no matter what appearance it may take, are where we derive most of our outlook on life. It can also be the main source of our early self-dialog. It can be the area in our lives where we look for role models on love and affection. With all the good that can come from the family, the responsibility is great to stay focused on the values of the group. Since the family is so crucial to most of us, we must handle these values with the utmost care and attention.

Not all families share the same values, and not all families work or function effectively. Today we hear the term "dysfunctional family." In terms of the Values Success program, a dysfunctional family is missing a common set of values, or a central purpose. This could also be a family that does have a clear vision but whose members do not all accept it. In families, like great sport teams, it is all or nothing. To develop a Value Statement for a family without all the family members input would be like asking your best friend to write your Personal Value Statement and Core Objectives on your behalf. Only the members of the family can write the Values Statement, because they have the enormous responsibility of carrying out its message and actions.

The first step in creating a family full of Valued Success is to create a Family Statement of Value.

The same rules apply to Family Values and Mission Statements as to individuals:

1. Take plenty of time to create the Family Statement of Value. The process can take a week, a few weeks, or many months to accurately reflect the families' true values.

2. List eight to ten bullet items to keep the family focused. In addition, the same time and care must be used in creating Family Value Statements as personal ones.

3. The Family Mission should be clear and concise, no more than one or two sentences.

The real advantage to creating a Family Statement of Values and Mission is that, depending on the size of the family, you have a built-in brainstorming group. If the family is large, you could choose representatives to voice a particular family perspective. As an example, younger children (age seven and under) could band together to express what they feel is important to the Family's Statement of Values. Then they may select one member to deliver their perspective to the entire family, thus insuring all members have input in the process. I would also encourage you to have all group members' sign or initial the document. This ensures all will be deeply committed to the values stated.

Next, you want to make the Family Statement of Values visible and accessible as a roadmap to all travelers (family members). Areas where the entire family meets and spends time together work best—maybe the kitchen, dining room, or family room. Alternatively, you can make framed copies for each bedroom in the home. Once you have created and positioned your statement of value, you are now ready to set Family Core Objectives.

Core objectives and strategic solutions are much more involved for families than for individuals, because you have so many more inputs than you do as an individual. The goal remains the same, as detailed in chapters two and three: you want input and agreement from all family members when setting the objectives and creating Statements of Value. When setting Family Core Objectives, I suggest a family meeting. The agenda for this gathering should be clear to everyone in the family. The family leaders can make or post an announcement to the group. For example,

---

Sample Announcement

"Mom and Dad would like to have a family meeting on Sunday to go over this years back to school game plan"

When setting Family Core Objectives, remember to stay focused on family values, not just personal ideals. This is a time when you are called to view an idea in terms of what is best for the families' value. Everyone must subordinate to the family, and no one member should be placed above or below its values. The reason I mention the words, below or above the family's value; is that often, one member tries to steer the family in a personal direction, acting as if he or she is above the process and the importance of the family's stated values. We must be aware of all members and look to those who don't feel included and are disengaging from the process. These members may act passively until it's time for action to accomplish objectives. Remember, in families, the all-or-nothing rule applies. Steven Covey, a bestselling author and a student of human behavior says, "We must not look for compromise in that 1 + 1 = something less than 2, but to come up with a synergistic approach in that 1 +

1 = something greater than 2."[25] Our families must work together to produce a synergistic effect when it pertains to Core Objectives and Valued Strategic Solutions.

As you move on to creating Valued Strategic Solutions, you'll find the family will move quickly from setting objectives to how it's going to get there. For instance, if a family set forth an objective to take a family vacation, in the next breath, everyone will probably be discussing locations, durations, whether the children will come, mode of travel, etc. All the above should be discussed when mapping out and planning a Family Valued Strategy. Often, the meeting to set objectives and strategies can be the done all at once.

Now your family is ready to implement a Valued Action, because of complexity of implementing one's own strategy vs. a plan with many family members, and be prepared for some challenges along the way. Just remember keep all the members of your family focused on their values and your chances for success increase.

In performing the Success Analysis, you need to evaluate the family using the following criteria:

1. Did the family collectively reach the objective?

---

25. Stephen R. Covey, *The 7 Habits of Highly Effective People* (New York: Simon and Schuster, 1989), 271.

2. Did the family continue to act according to its Statement of Value? If you can keep your family focused on its Value Statement, your family will experience many valued successes.

Corporations

Corporations are made up of many smaller groups (similar to family organizations), and these smaller groups are made up of many different individuals. Therefore, Valued Success program fits naturally within corporate structures. First, you have value-driven individuals, who then make up smaller groups driven by a central Statement of Values, and then you see a corporation made up with many individuals working in smaller groups towards a common Statement of Values and purpose.

Recently, I was watching a Sunday-morning politically oriented television program featuring Democrat and Republican leaders. As I watched, I thought, "I'm sure glad our companies and families today are not as politicized as our government has become—or are they?" All of us, at times, witness similar infighting and valueless actions in our everyday lives, either at work or in our families. I think it is fair to say that the most successful government administrations and corporations have had leadership focused on sending a clear valued message to their troops, who in turn took the appropriate Valued Actions. No one individual can produce a group or corporate success; only the members of the team or organization can by working together. There are many companies who impress me with their commitment to a central value, such as Wal-Mart. By asking each store associate to adopt an oath of friendliness, Wal-Mart has galvanized the entire company to the theme that the customer is number one. How many companies have we worked for or observed with a hidden corporate value, shared only among high-level management types? Quite a contrast to companies like Wal-Mart, which has chosen to share its value company-wide, down to the lowest-level store personnel.

In successful companies, the old adage "all or nothing" still applies. Just like in a family, in a company totally engaged to a common value and clearly defined corporate objectives, you will see a total Valued Success.

Companies with unclear or ever-changing missions or Statements of Value have no chance of keeping individuals with a strong sense of value and integrity. These companies usually have very high turnover rates and a crisis culture due to the lack of clear corporate value and direction.

Many books have been published on corporate excellence. This book was written for individuals, but I suggest that its principles and steps are effective in both a family and a business setting.

When setting Corporate Statements of Value, it is very difficult to get all employees involved in the process. What you can do is set up a committee using team members from all divisions and levels to ensure all areas are represented. The main point is to ensure clarity and to ease implementation. To reach the troops, remember Wal-Mart and its "The customer's number one" culture.

Try to see this exercise as the most important decision facing your company, because in fact, it is. Don't rush to define the culture and the value of the company. As when forming a Personal Values Statement, take time and plan many meetings for formulating these values.

Once you've created the Corporate Statement of Value and the company's Mission, share it with the entire company. This is the key step. When a Statement of Values is being implemented, it is crucial that all executive and middle managers spread the word to all employees and take only stated Valued Actions. One sure way to bring down a company is to say one thing and do another. The leadership of the company must have the corporate and personal integrity to act upon its values. This is what I feel truly represents corporate responsibility and separates the corporate winners from the losers.

Laminating pocket-sized cards with company credos, corporate values and mission statements is one way to share the value and culture with the entire organization. I'm sure there are many more creative means of getting your values and objectives out. So, make sure to use your entire team effectively to create the message and to get the word out.

After the Corporate Mission and Value Statements are set in place, it is time to address areas in the company or industry that need valued attention, of Core Corporate Objectives. This task should fall on the shoulders of the leadership of the organization and, like the Statement of Values, should be shared with all employees. Consider the internal and external aspects of the objective, also. One can be focused on some area of efficiency (external component) and another can be a positive cultural change your company seeks to improve upon (internal component).

Corporate Valued Strategic Solutions can and should be developed by all executive and mid-level management to insure a successful outcome; however, do not forget to get input from all areas and levels of the company.

No one employee has the sole responsibility to coordinate all creative thinking, not even the CEO. Companies like Wal-Mart have learned many valuable lessons from mid- to entry-level employees. It's no different to ask an individual to brainstorm on a particular issue and then opening up the discussion to a small group who can also come up with creative ideas; who do you think is going to come up with more ideas? Strong managers look for people who have different creative approaches to their corporate objectives. This is the same synergistic effect we looked for in families striving for a Valued Success. Remember, if we create a culture where only certain individuals have input to the process, we will soon run out of new and fresh ideas. Once their ideas run out, so does their corporate effectiveness. All great leaders look for individuals to step up and create a better company or environment. Nobody leads alone. Companies must strive for what I call *healthy diversity*—individual team members with various skills and talents working in the same valued framework. Getting employees to work creatively within the same corporate values and objectives is the most efficient way to manage any group.

Successful leaders, if some faction of the organization is not acting with a sense of value, either get the group or individuals acting on the firms value or they'll need transition out of the organization. Many effective leaders are fond of the expression "You are either part of the solution or you are part of the problem." My translation is, "You're either value-driven or you're gone." Harsh words, but a company that doesn't act with a sense of its own value is doomed to a valueless and problematic corporate culture. This reminds me of the following visualization: you are a foreman building a structure and all sub-contractors have a clear set of plans from which to work. The only issue is that not all the contractors view the details of the project the same way. As the leader of this endeavor, it is your responsibility to clear up any ambiguity concerning the details of the project. If you let the responsibility slide to other individuals, they will tailor the plans according to their personal interests. Example, they may value reducing costs, at all costs, which can be productive in some areas of construction but destructive in other areas. Each element (lighting, design, exteriors, plumbing, electrical) has to be planned carefully with regard to budget expenses. If not, the project will be less than successful. I suggest that's the reason many builders and contractors form relationships that last many years. Each party knows what to expect from the other, and they agree on how each element should be brought to completion. These strong partnerships are built upon similar working values and principles.

In being a part of any company, there is no more important ideal than taking Valued Actions. If you are a leader in any organization, set the company on a good foundation with a clear Mission and Corporate Statement of Value. All companies move in varied directions, however successful companies move in step with their values.

I will close by stating that there is certainly more to be said about how to make families and companies more successful, but nothing is more important to their health and success than acting with a clear sense of their own values.

Steven Covey, along with Roger and Rebecca Merrill, in their bestselling book *First Things First*, use the clock and the compass as symbols on the cover of the book. They write, "The clock represents our commitments, appointments, schedules, goals, activities—what we do with, and how we manage our time. The compass represents our vision, values, principles, mission, conscience, direction—what we feel is important and how we lead our lives."[26] They go on to discuss efficiency:

Efficiency, getting more done in less time. It makes good sense. We get more done. We reduce or even eliminate waste. We're streamlined. We're faster. We're leveraged. The increase in productivity is incredible. But the underlying assumption is that "more" and "faster" are better. Is that necessarily true? There's a vital difference between efficiency and effectiveness. You may be driving down the highway enjoying great traveling weather, and getting terrific mileage. You may be very efficient. But if you're headed south down the California coast on highway 101 and your destination is New York City—some three thousand miles to the East—you're not being very effective.[27]

Remember; use your Values and Mission Statements as your roadmap for effectiveness in a family or a business organization.

26. Stephen R. Covey, A. Roger Merrill, and Rebecca R. Merrill, *First Things First: To Live, to Love, to Learn, to Leave a Legacy* (New York: Simon and Schuster, 1994), 19.
27. Ibid., 26.

8

Valued Success Wrap-Up and Review

As I sit back and think about the essence of the principles and steps behind Valued Success, I am reminded of the inspiration for this book. Let me relay a story to you.

In my last semester of graduate school, I was enrolled in two classes. The first class was Corporate Strategy, the cornerstone course of the graduate business program taught by Dr. George Shagory, the department head. He was a University of Pennsylvania, Wharton School, MBA and received a Ph.D. from the University of Florida. After studying under him and doing the coursework, I came to believe that he was one of the most talented higher-level educators I'd known in all my years of schooling. Dr. Shagory led a class that was fully engaged, and everyone seemed to work independently, with a sense of interdependence. There was a synergy in our strategy and planning, looking at various companies during that semester.

The main purpose of the class was to study companies in the most fundamental way—evaluating missions, objectives, strategies, implementation of strategies, and review processes. As we studied particular companies, we were able to analyze their financial solvency, management structure, corporate culture, reporting systems, MIS/computer applications, and logistics. By doing this, we learned about how leaders today need to think in terms of developing and cultivating successful organizations.

That same semester I was also enrolled in a course entitled Group Dynamics. The course was based in communications and instructed by Michael Harton. He too was a gifted educator who brought a personal touch to the area of interpersonal communications. He also introduced me to some of Steven Covey's works, and with this I found Michael Harton to be a very enlightened, creative thinking educator. The first class in Group Dynamics was very interesting to me. The professor asked us to all relate a story and think deeply about a team that we felt worked effectively in our past, one that typified what good teams can do. I looked around at my classmates; while some of them struggled to think of something to relate, I thought for a moment and came up with a story that dated back to my eighth-grade basketball team in Michigan.

We were known as the Lake Orion West Chargers. We had a team of twenty young men who were driven and committed by our coach. Our coach was probably one of the strongest motivators and also understood the unlimited power of an effective team. We certainly weren't the most talented bunch, but at the center of this team were some very important values. We believed in the fundamentals of basketball. We believed that if we played at our fundamental best and worked diligently on the team defense, passing, shooting, and general skills, we could play with anyone. We believed that the team consisted of everyone. Our bench, our role players, our second- and third-team players, our starters and coaches, everyone was committed to helping each other become better each day and more focused around the team.

We each vowed to give our best, and more than that; we vowed to help one another be the best that we could be. When somebody struggled, it was the team's responsibility, along with the individual, to find a solution. No one piled on if someone was having trouble picking up a particular defensive read or missing an assignment. Our team was fully engaged in communicating effectively and helping that person to reach his highest potential.

With all that said and those values placed clearly in our minds, we set out with one Core Objective: if we could play together for an entire season and fully commit to one another in the fundamentals we aspired to, we had a chance to go undefeated that season. Coming off a season in seventh grade when we lost three games, and understanding how the teams in our league were far more talented, it seemed we had set a lofty goal.

Every person on that team felt that he was part of the winning. There were some team mates who didn't play very much, but our coach made everyone feel equally important and a part of each victory, no matter how big or small their contribution. He congratulated everyone and expressed the same confidence in every member of the team.

Another thing comes to mind about our team. When I came out of seventh grade, we had a person move into our community. He played the same position I did. In seventh grade, I was one of the better scorers on our team, and with this new teammate, a decision had to be made. It was decided that I would come off the bench and play a different role on the new eighth-grade team. The coach told me in a private meeting, "Paul, I need you to rebound the ball this year—I want you to feel that the most important thing you can do for our team's success is to come off the bench and ignite our rebounds on the defensive boards to secure the basketball, and to hit the glass on the offensive side to get our team time for second shot opportunities and slow down any counter attacks and fast-break attempts." I remember thinking, here's a coach who just clearly defined what he would like me to do, a Valued Strategy to help the team reach our Objective. I needed to work within the values that we had set: hard work, a team effort, and fundamentals, in my case concerning the skill of rebounding. There was a point that season when I felt a sense of victory and personal contentment each time I got a rebound, because I was working for the value of the team. Although I was not scoring all the points or grabbing the assists, by doing the work the team needed I felt valued and honored. It was a great lesson in life witnessing how our coach treated each role player. He treated each one with dignity and helped him understand his contributions to the team; with all that, he made the team feel unified and strong. A word I like to use is *engaged*, a feeling that everyone is involved and conscious of the efforts that are going on. No one is sitting on the fence. Everyone is in the game doing whatever necessary to make the win happen.

As I sat back that day in Michael Harton's class, I thought I had never been part of a team where I had made such an impact. I had never felt as much joy as going through an entire season, sometimes with two practices a day or on weekends; feeling so much fulfillment that I, along with the rest of the team, stayed true to our values and worked hard in what we believed in. We accomplished something.

If we had lost another three games that season, I would have still felt a great sense of contentment knowing that we had worked within our values, had a central purpose, and felt good about what we did. But as it turned out, our team went undefeated in eighth grade. We all sat in our locker room and the coach very emotionally stated that he was very proud of us, that the community was very proud, and that we should be proud of one another. I think I was most grateful that this coach showed all of us and we showed each other that together, driven by the same set of principles and values, we were a very empowered group of young men. For us, the lesson was not that our talent was measured; but in our ability to engage our values unilaterally was only true measure of accomplishment.

In that class, I started to think, wow, what made this team wonderful and the experience so fulfilling was the element of personal and team value, things that I believed we all shared on that team. Then I realized that many of the corporations I had observed were missing the element of corporate value or purpose. If those companies, or more importantly the individuals in those companies, developed a sense of value while incorporating a sound corporate strategy, a winning combination would result. Thus, if we review the key business principles of mission, objectives, strategy, implementation, and review and then compare it against the Valued Success Formula; we'll see the only real difference is the importance we are placing on value in every phase of the plan.

Valued Success Formula

1. Values and Mission Statements

2. Core Objectives

3. Valued Strategic Solutions

4. Taking Valued Actions

5. Success Analysis

That was the inspiration for this program, along with tireless study into human behavior, corporate cultures, and many books about personal development and success. I learned a great deal about success from likes of Dale Carnegie, Steven Covey, Anthony Robbins, Mark McCormick, Denis Waitley, and Zig Ziglar, among others, who all have messages I found to be insightful and engaging. However, each had a particular expertise. Zig Ziglar and Anthony Robbins are tremendous motivators. Their strength is in their communication and being able to define how people can expect more from their lives. Steven Covey's work, probably the most similar to the Valued Success approach, is a very important look at seven habits of highly effective people.[28] And lastly, there are many books on interpersonal communications that teach how to be a more effective communicator, such as Dale Carnegie's *How to Win Friends and Influence People* and Mark McCormick's *What They Still Don't Teach You at Harvard Business School.*

I learned many things from these books and others, but what I ultimately gained from these works was this: if you are able to put your values at the forefront of your decisions and your actions, you will have a much more enjoyable, satisfying, and fulfilling life. I hope the Valued Success program is a clear and not-too-cumbersome approach to

---

28. Covey, *7 Habits*, 53.

creating a less complicated, more value-driven life. I hope Valued Success lets you free yourself up to live in accordance with the values that you set forth.

My impression is that everyone, day to day, is faced with questions of which direction to go, which decisions to make, and how to make them. I suggest that it is nearly impossible to go through life making decisions without a sense of what we truly value.

Let us now review one last time the principles of Valued Success. In Valued Success, the first three principles comprise the framework of the program (our roadmap). In step one; we establish both Mission and Values Statements to work on developing what your true values are. I suggest you use a bullet list, with ten items or fewer, to clearly state what you value in life, who you are, and what you aspire to be. I have provided some exercises on how to get to these important personal values.

The second part of the book discusses setting Core Objectives, which I define as the areas in our lives that need our valued attention. The reason I say valued attention is that it makes no sense to work on objectives or goals that do not relate to your values. They are outside the framework of what you believe. Also, when setting Core Objectives, make sure you get down to the root causes as opposed to mere symptoms.

In step three, we laid out ideas to create Valued Strategic Solutions. Valued Solutions take brainstorming, modeling, and looking at individuals you admire and value. At this stage, the challenges are similar to those of setting Core Objectives.

Once you have defined who you are and what you believe, the direction you would like to go, and the means to get there through your values, you will have your personal roadmap. I would call this a *position of alignment.* There's a term in music, resonance, which describes musical notes put together in a chord structure. This could be used as a metaphor for the internal alignment we've just discussed, a strategy based on similar values and Core Objectives based on issues you can affect through your actions. The opposite of that in music theory is dissonance. Dissonance is defined as "a harsh or disagreeable combination of sounds; discord."[29] The sounds are out of alignment. Dissonance in our program is internal misdirection. You either don't have a sense of who you are, or you have no strategy to reach any goals, because you've never given much thought to what you believe in. Any plans you implement or strategies you develop are probably the result of a reactive state—a state of mind in which you are simply reacting to outside stimuli without any thought about your core values.[30]

The first three steps make up the most important content of the program. These concepts involve knowing

29. American Heritage Dict.
30. Covey, *7 Habits,* 68.

who you are, where you are going, and how to get there. Nothing is more powerful than that in any person's life.

In the fourth step, once you've laid out your strategies and set your Core Objectives, you must take Valued Actions. In your actions, you are responsible for acting with the same integrity you've shown in developing your plan. By taking Valued Actions you will feel contentment, success, comfort, and joy—the same engaging, elated feeling I had while playing basketball in eighth grade.

Finally, in the fifth and final step of the Valued Success program, you will have a chance to review your plan's success. This is where your Success Analysis begins. Did you actually get what you wanted in terms of results (the external component)? Did you work the way you set out to work, within your values? Did you act with a sense of who you are and what you truly believe in (the internal component)?

After the fifth step, we talked about the effects of having a positive mental attitude, the importance of having a consistent belief in the power of a positive outcome. Having strong faith in your ability to work through any issue with a sense of empowerment concerning what is possible is part of a positive mental approach.

We also looked at how the Valued Success program helps not only individuals but families and corporations.

Putting together my ideas and acquired knowledge to write this book has been one of the most fulfilling experiences in my life. It has allowed me to express ideas that I hope will bring you a truly Valued Success and a lifetime of Valued Successes.

I want to thank my family and friends for supporting me through the years. A project like this book took time away from some people I value most, so in completing this work I feel a great sense of love and pride to the people who continue to support me in my journey to be even more value driven.

Lastly, please note that 20% of all profits from the sale of this book will support the following noble causes:

- *Juvenile Diabetes Research Foundation*
- *National Association for Autism Research*
- *The Rodman Ride for Kids*
- *Dana-Farber Cancer Institute*

More Highlights from Valued Success ...

- There is nothing in this universe worth selling out the true values and principles to which you hold dear. No amount of money, power, or fame is more important than your principles.

- How can you go through life without your own customized roadmap? How can you be expected to make life's tough choices without the ability to access your personal core values roadmap? That is the purpose of a Values Statement.

- By writing down your strategy, your chances for success are much greater.

- The more complex you make your plan, the more difficult it will be to accomplish your goals or achieve any Valued Successes.

- It makes no sense to set an objective for which you are either ill prepared or incapable of completing.

- Make sure your strategy is realistic and you have all the proper resources to meet the Core Objectives.

- Only through Valued Actions can we say that our ideas and solutions have truly worked.

- You must push negative thoughts aside and concentrate deeply on creating a positive self-dialog—envision a positive outcome, over and over.

- These values exist whether you write them down or not. The reason for getting them down on paper is to help individuals and corporations more readily access them.

- With our power to think positively comes the resource of our personal potential.

- We have the power to choose our response to any situation.

- Take a bad situation and create opportunities to learn; take a good situation and create even higher expectations of success.

- Only in a company totally engaged to common values and clearly defined corporate objectives can you see total Valued Success.

Bibliography

Blanchard, Ken, and Don Shula. *Everyone's a Coach*. Audiotape. Harper Audio, 1995.

Brown, H. Jackson, *A Father's Book of Wisdom*. Nashville, TN: Rutledge Hill Press, 1988.

Carnegie, Dale. *How to Win Friends and Influence People*. New York: Simon & Schuster, 1981.

Carruth, Gorton, and Eugene Ehrlich. *American Quotations*. New Jersey: Wings Books, 1992.

Churchill, Winston.

Churchill in His Own Voice.

Laurence Olivier and John Gielgud, narrators. Courtesy of Carl Foreman and the British Broadcasting Corporation. The Rise and Fall of the Third Reich, by William L. Shirer, Simon & Schuster, 1959, 1960.

Caedmon Audio, CPN2018. Audio cassette.

Clifton, Donald O., and Paula Nelson. *Soar With Your Strengths*. New York: Delacorte Press, 1992.

Covey, Stephen, R., Roger A. Merrill, and Rebecca R. Merrill. *First Things First*. New York: Simon & Schuster, 1994.

Covey, Stephen, R. *7 Habits of Highly Effective People*. New York: Simon & Schuster, 1989.

————. *Principle-Centered Leadership*. New York: Summit Books, 1990.

McCormack, Mark H. *What They Still Don't Teach You at Harvard Business School*. New York: Bantam Books, 1989.

Nixon, Richard, M. *In The Arena*. New York, Simon & Schuster, 1990.

Peale, Dr. Norman Vincent. *The Power of Positive Thinking*. Audiotape. Simon & Schuster Sound Ideas, 63530-1, 1995.

Riley, Pat. *The Winner Within*. New York: G.P. Putnam's Sons, 1993.

Robbins, Anthony. *Awaken the Giant Within*. New York: Simon & Schuster, 1991.

———. *Unlimited Power*. New York: Ballantine Books, 1986.

Shaugnessy, Dan. *Evergreen: The Boston Celtics*. New York: St. Martin's Press, 1990.

The American Heritage Dictionary, Second College Edition. Boston, Massachusetts: Houghton Mifflin Company, 1982.

Thompson, Arthur A., Jr., and A. J. Strickland III. *Strategic Management: Concepts and Cases*, 6th ed. Homewood, IL: Irwin Inc., 1992.

Waitley, Denis. *Being the Best*. Audio cassette. Nightingale-Conant Audio, 712CT.

Walton, Sam, and John Huey. *Made in America: My Story*. New York: Doubleday, 1992.

Ziglar, Zig. *How to Be a Winner*. Audio cassette. Simon & Schuster, 52063-6., 1995.

———. *Secrets of Closing the Sale*. New York: Berkley Books, 1982.

978-0-595-71389-9
0-595-71389-0

Printed in the United States
109071LV00004B/1-99/P